It's Time

For Mary-Ann & Tony
with love & admiration,

Doris

10-24-98

IT'S TIME

poems by Doris Abramson

Haley's
Athol, Massachusetts

Haley's
Post Office Box 248
Athol, Massachusetts   01331
1.800.215.8805

ACKNOWLEDGMENTS
    Grateful acknowledgment is made to the following publications:
    University of Utah, Graduate School of Social Work, Salt Lake City, *Affilia, Journal of Women and Social Work,* Volume 6, Number 3, Fall, 1991: "Eubie Blake and My Father" and "A Visit to the Nursing Home"
    The Evergreen Chronicles, Volume IV, No. 1, Fall, 1988: "On Hearing of the Death of an Ex-lover"
    Hatch-Billops Collection, Inc., New York, N.Y., *Artist & Influence,* XV, 1996: "Josephine Baker and Fanny Brice"
    University of Massachusetts, Amherst, Massachusetts, *The Massachusetts Review,* XXXVII, Summer, 1996: "What Does She Read?" Reprinted from *The Massachusetts Review,* ©1996 The Massachusetts Review, Inc.

Library of Congress Cataloging-in-Publication Data:
Abramson, Doris E.
    It's time : poems / by Doris Abramson.
        p.   cm.
    ISBN 1-884540-40-6
    I. Title
 PS3551.B718177   1998
    811'.54--dc21   98-37688
                                                                                        CIP

For Dorothy

Contents

a Foreword to It's Time

by Anne Halley

I thought of beginning with the extraordinary circumstance that a young woman of Scandinavian extraction, growing up in Amherst in the '30s and '40s, should have written her first poem from the point of view of a black man who has just witnessed a lynching. In that poem, the student Doris Abramson showed an empathy and concern, an awareness of problematic history and of others that might well be called surprising.

Doris Abramson's poems still surprise me. Her texts never go to conclusions that their beginnings might lead me to expect; the unpredictability—at least to me—of these poems, and their often miniature strangeness, is a distinct virtue. I mean, the directions of thought and feeling, the turns these poems take on the way to conclusion are *sui generis*. The texts go *this* poet's way, and no others'.

Although the poems look easy, like notations that concern the events of a peaceful daily existence (a ball game on the Common, say, ladybugs in the garden, a visit to a friend in a nursing home, a performance witnessed, or—after all something momentous—a death), they are not as transparent—or simple—as they might at first appear. For instance, on page seven, *Solitary Dancer*.

Let me be pedantic for a moment, only to point out how much can be going on in a small text. This particular poem invokes a classic dramatic situation: someone sees an odd, inexplicable human event and describes it. There is another observer, more knowledgeable, an Authority, present on the scene as well. The innocent turns to Authority to ask "Why?" Authority gives its usual answer, *Because...* Unwilling or unable to accept that answer, the questioner must formulate her own.

The traditional dialogic structure behind the poem helps it to reverberate. The text, however, performs its own, surprising turn. Although one authority is subverted in the pattern of the poem, the text suggests that the dancer has still to meet interference—maybe something worse—from a less well-meaning other.

Reading the poem, we share the speaker's wonder when the firm, thoughtful woman, who is acquainted with the man, says that he is "dancing with himself." She appears to account for his eccentric public behavior—the solitary circling, first one way and then the other—by describing him as "very bright—but homeless." Neither characteristic answers the question "Why?" which the poem's speaker, in apparent innocence, first posed.

One thing, then, that the poem tells us is that the answers we get don't comport well with questions we need to have answered. Although the structure of the stanzas might lead one, next, to expect a better answer than the one Authority had given—"firmly, thoughtfully"—in stanza two, the next stanza goes on to another question, and so implies that perhaps there are no firm answers, only some that sound as if they were. "As if that were all," the poem says. It's not.

Dancing *with* yourself is different from dancing *by* yourself, and in a public place the former, I submit, is a good deal stranger than the latter. People who dance *with* themselves when they are not *by* themselves may suggest other, more alarming, forgetful-of-propriety, behaviors. And the myth of self-loving Narcissus ends with the intervention of a punishing god.

The poem's final question—"Until who or what, I wonder, cuts in"—calls up, first, a dance floor where partnerless stags "cut in" on couples to replace one of the partners (usually, if I remember correctly, the passive follower is handed over to the new leader). Cutting in on a dancing couple interrupts a pattern and an established rhythmic relationship and has overtones (undertones?) of sexual competition for a prize, self-assertion, hostility. Think of all the old movies in which the phrase "may I cut in?" signals an impending confrontation, which may or may not be followed by a fist fight, a general free-for-all, or the film's happy end. So the poem's ultimate term begins a denouement wondered about—not included—in the poem.

We know that this Narcissus, who is dancing with himself, will surely be intruded on—as strange couples in stories must always be, before the story can end, either happily or the other way. Cut in on by a rude bystander, or a well-meaning caseworker, or a god, the awakened dancer will be cut off from himself, inevitably, and—as is the fate not only of narcissi—cut down. The poem, which takes an observed performance as its starting point, is itself a performance that moves "in little circles,/calculated ones . . . turned gracefully . . ."

Another poem I like for its double-edged performance is *Josephine Baker and Fanny Brice*, which evokes performers, their acts, and something of the strangeness of show-business selves and self-presentations. We know these female performers from film images, from books, photographs and records: we know their legends, feel their auras; we know them by having seen them impersonated by contemporary stars and aspirants to stardom; they have become cultural goods, material, even texts, to be read and interpreted, broken down, reassembled.

The poem reassembles the two women as performers at the Follies (in New York? in Paris?), meeting "in passing"—signaling to each other with winks, smirks, and crossed eyes, "outrageously . . . mirroring each other's audacity . . . comic queens rashly strutting their stuff." According to the poem, Brice performed in black face; Baker, the black woman (this is not in the poem), sometimes worked in a costume of bananas. The poem's question, "Did they share bits of business knowingly?" leads to the penultimate sentence: "The questions go on and on."

Open-endedness is typical of these poems. This text will not tell how far to go in questioning—but it encourages a reader to push beyond its conclusion: for instance, *as what* did Brice and Baker "pass"? Who or what were they, really, these females, these impersonators, impersonating broad comedic female types and behaviors? The poem makes us wonder—maybe giggle and mug a little in imagination, trying on what roles we might try to "pass" in—but again the text gives no firm answer, no prescription: if a secret is hinted at and signaled, none is revealed.

Other poems I like especially are *Eubie Blake and My Father, Rosa, Caesar, Danse Macabre,* and *What Does She Read?* I like them for the turns they take, the scenes they perform, the questions they refuse to answer with any finality. All the poems, however, raise questions of how to perceive dailiness; they can startle a reader, can push and prod consciousness (gently, quietly) to go some steps farther, to take a new turn in an unfamiliar direction. Doris Abramson's empathic concerns and awareness are as striking now, as full of surprises, as her first poem promised.

an Introduction to It's Time

by Doris Abramson

When I was about ten years old, my grandmother asked me, "What do you want to be when you grow up?" I remember the moment, where I stood and where she sat in our parlour. I answered—as I recall, without hesitation—"A poet."

"A poet!" She laughed and shook her head in what was obviously disapproval. Where did I get such an idea, she wanted to know. I answered her scorn immediately, telling her that we had been learning about Emily Dickinson in school. As I started to tell her about this great poet who had lived in my home town, she interrupted.

"Em-il-y Dick-in-sohn," she said in her measured Swedish accent, sneering on each syllable. "I know all about *her. Sure,* she's the one who wrote a lot of poems and let other people make money on them after she was dead. Em-il-y Dick-in-sohn. Ha!"

I left the room in tears. No one laughed at Emily Dickinson. Not in Amherst. Not in 1935.

Perhaps in part to spite my grandmother, I wrote poems in high school, the kind of poems that rhymed neatly and had more than their fair share of leaves that whispered, Love with a capital "L," and suffering, oh, lots of suffering. I didn't call myself a poet; I just wrote poems now and then.

As an undergraduate at Massachusetts State College (Mass State College, soon to be UMass, Amherst), I was challenged by a remarkable teacher, Leonta Horrigan, who had her class in Modern Poetry (Whitman to Eliot) try to write poems in order to get a feel of what it takes to do such a thing. The first assignment was to write a short poem in rhymed couplets. Following is the poem I wrote to fulfill that assignment more than fifty years ago:

Black Brother

A big black man was hanged from that green tree.
The crowd was loud and pushing close to see.
He found his death against the graying sky,
And eyes were wise that did not choose to cry.
If I were white and strong, I could complain.
But silent, black, I saw my brother slain.

I remember that I had read in a newspaper that Negroes had to be stoical at a lynching for fear of having the lynchers' wrath turn on them. I tried to imagine being black and being present at the lynching of my brother. I've learned over the years that it's better to write from one's own experience—or at least from one's own possibly imagined experience. I'm not ashamed of the poem; it fulfilled the assignment and shows an awareness of another's pain. Also, the leaves don't whisper, and the suffering is not an abstraction.

Miss Horrigan also had us memorize poems. My earlier teachers did, too. I learned Dickinson and Frost and Millay poems by heart. (Isn't that a wonderful expression, "by heart"? Is it used any other way?) Having those poets in my bloodstream was a great gift to any writing I've done since, in prose or verse. Also, local poet Robert Francis was my violin teacher when I was in junior high school. I read his poems, and I enjoyed listening to the cadences of his gentle talk.

It's only now that I realize how much it meant to me to grow up in Amherst, among poets living and dead, studying with teachers who made good use of their melodies. Miss Fleming, Miss Weeks, Miss Horrigan, they all brought poetry into my life. And they led me, by example, by their creative assignments, to my career as a teacher.

Even when I was doing graduate work in theater history, I always managed to take courses in what had come to be called the oral interpretation of literature (earlier, in a more prescriptive period, it had been elocution). First Miss Sickels, at Smith College, then Miss Kramer, at Columbia University, helped me to find ways to use my voice and speech to communicate works of literature to an audience. These speech teachers made the analysis of a poem, the search for meaning, a pleasure. There was, of course, the motivation of performance.

I realize that I have called all my teachers Miss. That was their title in the thirties, the forties, even the fifties. Not Professor. Certainly not Doctor, although a couple possessed that title. They were Miss, and so was I when I began to teach in the mid fifties. By the late sixties, I was Doris. Another world.

In the thirty-four years that I taught at the University of Massachusetts at Amherst, I directed plays, taught theater history, dramaturgy, and oral interpretation courses—and I wrote a poem now and then. I was fortunate during those years to have poets among my friends: Anne Halley, Jimmy Merrill, Michelle Cliff, Adrienne Rich, Robert Francis, Leon Barron, Bob Tucker, Joe Langland, Stan Koehler, Dave Clark, Arnold Kenseth, John Ratti. Francis, Kenseth, and Ratti all invited me to read their poems on the radio, on WFCR. I liked the challenge of being a stand-in for these poets. Different voices had to be produced to match the meanings of their poems. I thought of myself as principally a performer, in the medieval sense a minstrel to be called upon to sing another's songs. To this day, I mostly think of myself that way.

When did I start to take myself at all seriously as a poet, to write poems in earnest? When I retired from teaching in 1987. I didn't sit down and say, "O.K., time to write poems." Because I had the time, maybe, I wrote poems that I worked on more than usual. I showed most of them to Anne Halley, a few to Jimmy Merrill and Michelle Cliff. They were all encouraging, kind but specific in their criticism.

All the poems in this collection have been written since 1987. Looking at them, I realize that my dear mother is not represented. My domineering grandmother, yes, my father whom I scarcely knew, but not my mother. I have found it difficult to put her into words. Perhaps they will come in time.

Shortly before she died in 1961, I did write a poem that I believe now to have come out of my fear of her dying. At the time I thought I was writing about a man who is told that his wife is dying. (Talk about distancing.) I thought of it as a comment on language—on talk, really. Mister A. hasn't words to talk about loss, not the big loss, death.

Love Poem

"Your wife is dying, Mister A."
"*So.*
So are we all."
"You know what I mean.
Soon.
She's going soon."
"*I know.*
I had to say it a way I could take it."
"Oh."
  Then silence,
  a silence of despair.
  Hope had hummed in the elevator.
  But hope was gone,
  Gone from this white room.
"*My wife is dying.*"
"So are we all."
"*I know.*"

I had forgotten all about this poem until I had written

"Alzheimer Moment" in 1994. They are in a similar oblique style, in short words, in dialogue. "Love Poem" came out of fear, "Alzheimer Moment"—and also "A Visit to the Nursing Home"—probably out of gratitude for what my mother was spared.

In May of 1997, I was invited to read some of my own poems publicly, for the Arnold Kenseth Poetry Series in South Amherst. The announcement in *The Daily Hampshire Gazette* referred to "Poet Doris Abramson." That came as quite a shock. Remembering how I answered my grandmother's question all those years ago, I might have said that, in my seventy-third year, I had grown up at last. It's time.

Dream House

Remember the house we looked at, studied to think we might own?
We measured the rooms, dreamed the furnishings, paced out places
to share our lives. Remember planning a table by a window
where a table hadn't been before? We knew from shadings on the floor
it had been elsewhere, not in the light as we saw it. Walking
from parlour to dining room, from there to rooms and rooms beyond,
we imagined Windsor chairs, pillowed couches, even portraits
on the walls. And that's not all: we saw what things would rest
on small shelves—odd baubles of glass, photos framed and propped,
china eggs—and felt our rugs under foot where now no rugs lay.

For one day—oh, for many days if truth be told—
that house was ours though elegant beyond our owning.
We could furnish it, could feel it, could all but possess
     a house that in dreams is forever ours.

For Dorothy in Early November

Yellow mums on the window sill in a cobalt blue vase,
an early Christmas cactus starting to blossom
in a Bennington bowl, red geraniums bright among
bits of evergreen in a mottled gray dish.
These are her offerings to the household gods this day,
and they are spectacular—in a minimalist way.
They are what came to hand to please the eye.

I sing the praises of a woman who knows
how to use yellow and blue, red and green,
in a room already alive with the color of love.

My Grandmother

My grandmother furnished her house
with an eye to selling it, never cared about
or sentimentalized even a corner of a room,
and yet it looked for all the world
as if it meant something to her.
Not at all. When she'd finished each detail—
it seemed lovingly—she sold what
from the beginning meant only money
to her. She lived in a house as long
as it took her to arrange it for another
for profit. Perfectly simple, convenient, neat,
indisputable in her scheme of things.

Like stage sets rooms were prepared
for buyers. Colors and fabrics and lines
were chosen for a time when someone
would come to admire and agree to buy.
I remember asking, "Don't you love that chair?"
only to hear her laugh at such an idea.
"Love a chair!" It's a lesson well offered,
not to love things, but huddled in the dark
in a saleable bed, I hugged my doll close
and knew I loved things, though transient,
more than I loved my cool grandmother.

Solitary Dancer

He took a few steps,
then turned round and round
in a circle. Sometimes one way,
sometimes the other. In little circles,
calculated ones. He turned gracefully,
arrhythmically but prettily.

He was, a woman said who knew him
from daily encounters at the store,
"dancing with himself." Why?
She said firmly, thoughtfully,
"He's very bright—but homeless."
As if that were all.

He moved past expressionless,
turning, shutting out the day.
Bright and homeless he dances
with himself in little circles—
until who or what, I wonder,
cuts in.

Growing Up in Connecticut

My friend Betsy stopped playing tennis
when she saw her neighbor Kate playing
across the way, slender and powerful.
Who could compete with that?
She wouldn't even try.

She saw Kate Hepburn young,
long before we did on the silver screen,
however much it cost her of a game
she wishes at eighty she'd played.

Josephine Baker and Fanny Brice

When Baker and Brice met at the Follies,
did they wink in passing? Did they smirk
as they worked their magic on the crowd,
crossing their eyes outrageously, grinning
and mirroring each other's audacity?
Brice came first. Was Baker a copy cat?
Did they share bits of business knowingly,
comic queens rashly strutting their stuff?
Did Baker see Brice in blackface? Did she laugh?
The questions go on and on. The answers left
when they left, clowning over, exits made.

Pedagogy

"Miss Potter has a rubber hose!" we children sang.
I never saw it, never knew anyone who had. It was
enough she was said to have one. She was feared,
obeyed at once by children caught dreaming—perhaps
of year's end and being promoted to Miss Fleming's class.
Ah, Miss Fleming, whose beauty prompted attention
and encouraged deeds no rubber hose real or imagined
could elicit from children. We'd be attentive then,
ready to serve, perhaps even ready to learn—next year.

Teaching and Being Taught

for Hallie Flanagan Davis

How it hurt Hallie that Alger Hiss acted as he did,
not as he looked or seemed. "The end of life is an action,"
she said, teaching us Greek drama, only mentioning Hiss
in passing.
       A grainy photo of an earnest man in a felt hat
       was all he was to me then. Later, reading, I
       learned more. Still, yesterday's lies and
       yesterday's truths continue to confuse.
I do believe
that he made the difference in what I learned
from a look that crossed my teacher's face.
Comparing art and life effortlessly, she taught us
basics that day: "'The end of life is an action,
not a quality,' Aristotle wrote." And Hallie was faced
with the fear she'd believed in a man whose looks
she approved, whose ways were seemingly right
but actively, critically wrong. That personal moment,
that parenthetical name, taught me much about acting
and living and—most of all—about teaching and being taught.

What Does She Read?

What does she read,
the Gish look-alike in a corner booth,
holding a paperback close to her eyes?
The book's thin, always easy to hold
with title concealed. Looking around it
at times, she takes us in taking her in daily.

Wearing a fur-trimmed cloche one day,
a broad-brimmed hat another, wearing
rings upon rings, she makes the diner
her theater. And she knows how to pose.

Passing her I lower my eyes
for fear of blurting *Hello*.
The agreement here is to eat
together yet apart.
But what does she read? Poems? What?
Slim novels by Beverly Nichols or Virginia Woolf?
De Musset? Dickinson? Collected stories of
Chekhov? Shakespeare's plays?

When I dream of her, I dream her younger—
sometimes Dorothy, sometimes Lillian Gish—
in a white dress, in a boat rowed by me,
while she reads under a parasol
from a book I cannot see.

Dickinson in Harlem

"Will there really be a Morning?" they sang,
The Boys Choir of Harlem sang, "Is there such a thing
as Day?"—twenty years ago asking questions
posed by a poet a century before. Little black boys
with eager eyes climbed the scales urgently, singing
with sweet, unchanged voices. And I wonder now
what kind of morning came, what sort of day
for those boys grown to men in our time.

Boys Who Will Soon Be Men

Boys who will soon be men
play ball across from my house
on grass that is theirs by eminent domain.
I hear them talk. They boast of fathers,
excuse sisters, at times, and seem
to avoid the subject of mothers
(too questionable to be talked of here).

They preen—for each other,
not for me, a maiden lady on her porch.
Oh, these boys who will soon be men
mean business when they throw
and miss, and throw again
hard balls in a game that
will soon be life to them.

While I sit quietly watching
boys who will always be boys
playing one game one way
(to my happy exclusion), I smile
in anticipation of their surprise
when rules change with time
and games go past catch and throw.

Home

"I'm home! I'm home!"
a small voice cried
reaching home from third.
"Throw home!"
"Home!"
"Throw home again!"
"Second!"
"Home!"
Highest, most plaintive,
the cry of "Home! I'm home!"

These little ones
make up the rules
of a game they know
only vaguely,
just enough to cry
"Home! I'm home!"
just enough to tag—
"Throw home"—
and run and slide
where bases ought to be.

His Second Wife

His second wife paled, the first and third
    being vivid.
She stood at parties, beautiful, collected,
    and cool.
And no one asked, "Who's she?"
No connection was made between her and him
    or anyone.
She left no imprint on the social scene.
But she was always there as if trying to be
    noticed,
      wanting to be given her place
      in the hierarchy of his wives.

We Watched

In the Fifties there was one at every academic party:
the mad wife who wouldn't be kept home or upstairs or
anywhere but where she'd speak her piece, spill a drink,
wave a finger close to a nose, tell stories to contradict
the occasion. Yes, we were known to call her a witch.
She'd dance and trip and blame, of course, the one who'd
brought her. "No grace, no balls," I heard one say
of her husband as they waltzed. He was praised for coping
and blamed for the same—saint and sap, one man.

We watched. Social voyeurs, we enjoyed taking sides;
though allegiances shifted as the scenes were played.
Obviously, she needed him, and he needed her. Perhaps
both needed us—an audience of their peers.

Danse Macabre

In Madagascar they dig up the dead to dance with them,
swing them in sacks, rocking them to and fro,
rejoicing to reclaim their own, their families,
to dance with them heartily—before making new shrouds
and returning death's prize to its place in earth.
(Many are Christians and believe in the Resurrection.)
Those who sleep on the old shrouds, we're told,
    are in search of fertility. The skulls
      on the tombstones smile in anticipation.
In Madagascar they dig up the dead to dance with them.
    We do the same, but in dreams.

A Visit to the Nursing Home

It took me a moment to see
what she held was her teeth,
false teeth like castanets in her
bony hand. "Like a painting by Goya,"
I thought, and moved on, hoping
to find the object of my visit
alert this day, awake to my presence—
if not welcoming, not mocking or sad.
(There's no way to prepare for
the moods of the very old.)

She was quiet except to speak
of drowning, then looked as puzzled
as I was by her words. After a while
she broke a long silence, saying clearly,
"I never meant to stay so long."
I wept, my back to her, at the window.
She had it right. No one wants
to stay so long that she drowns
without knowing what to drown really means.

It's Time

I put his scarf in my drawer today
—one year since the day he died.
It's been mine all this time, but now
I've claimed it, made it part of
what I'll wear, made it something
I'll turn to, knowing it's there
in my bureau, with gloves, with other
scarves I've worn for years. He left
a year ago, but only today I find
by placing one thing he's worn among
     my things, my ordinary ornaments,
     I've brought him back—and now can
     let him go.

Had They Lived

in memory of Ted and John

Had they lived to be the old men they so resembled
at their untimely end, how different it would have been
for them and for us their survivors, relatives and friends.
They would have gathered more things and assigned them
differently at a later demise. Another generation would be
gathering plates and lamps and lustre ware, sofas
and chairs, rugs, for homes not even imagined now.

As it was, fading into death slowly, inexorably,
they urged us to take things away, noted our tears—
all so near in age and sympathy and now in sadness—
and planned our homes to reflect their presence in years
to come. They took what time they had to reassure us
at the end.

Ted

1.

He was upstairs dying while life bustled below.
Dogs barked, children cried, and he died.
"That's life," he may have thought.
Sun rose, sun set, and he died.
Life went on—without him.

2.

The trees I see today
he no longer sees.

3.

Did you see that bit of wind
run across the grass?
Did you see the grass respond?

Denis,

I think of you
every day
at sunset
when I look at a scene
out my window
like one you gave me
in an Irish painting
that matches
my New England trees
    and lawns
      and distant buildings.

Gray
the tree trunks loom
and lawns are green
are gold
at our sunset,
yours and mine.

Your sun's set,
my friend,
mine's here alive
and I've this reminder:
my eye's view
and a gift given
perhaps to say
    you'd stay
      in blessed memory.

Did Judith Anderson Die? (1990)

Did Judith Anderson die,
and I didn't notice?
    Cathleen Nesbitt—who
was engaged to Rupert Brooke
when but a girl—Cathleen Nesbitt
finally died. And Garbo,
who asked to be *let* alone,
died the other day.
Perhaps the noble Dame
had the bad fortune to die
the day a Wall came down.
Or when a shuttle was launched
successfully. On such days
we tend to miss obits.

Or maybe she hasn't died at all.
    Dietrich hasn't. Say—
what about Ina Claire?
Dame Edith Evans has gone,
leaving the fine art
of the arched eyebrow
to Maggie Smith. (Who,
I wonder, wears her clothes?)
LeGallienne's still here
and still in voice
I'm told. But her pals
are mostly on the other side:
Tallulah, Margaret, and—
after a long ride—Estelle.

What of Judith Anderson,
housekeeper and Queen?
Does she bark her lines in
Santa Barbara still? Or has
she moved on? Oh, I can wait
to know. Postponement is,
after all, a kind of keeping.

Eubie Blake and My Father

I longed to touch
Eubie Blake's head,
to feel the skull
beneath the silky skin.

Perhaps because
my father died
in his prime,
thick hair still growing,

I wanted to know
what I'd missed:

the skull that shows
the way we'd like to go—worn out, used,
songs all sung
and dances danced.

My father went
in the heat of an accident,
on a cold night,
much left undone.

He went suddenly
to ashes,
Eubie gradually
to bone.

Deprived of touching either,
I feel oddly alone.

On Hearing of the Death of Douglass Watson

When the patriarch of our soap opera died
we cried and cried, much as we had
at the deaths of our own dear dads.
For we had chosen Mac Cory; he was ours
at two every weekday afternoon. He'd never
disappointed us. Kind, forgiving, sometimes
maligned, he was godlike among petty men,
either present or predictably in the wings
ready to save the day for all of us.

Now that the actor's gone—and with him Mac—
to whom will we turn on bright and rainy afternoons?

Virginia's Book

She knew
(she was dying)
she knew
they would never
be set up again,
but she wrote
on the fly leaf
(handed the book
to me): "To be
held in trust
until the day
the old bookshelves
are set up again."
    Not in this world.
She knew
she was dying,
and I wonder still
what she dreamed
of another Time.
I have the book
(Does it matter?
Under A Glass Bell
by Anaïs Nin.)
and her note.
She has the Time I
will meet in time.
For now, amen.
    And then, Amen.

On Hearing of the Death of an Ex-Lover

Now that she's ashes, and I'm old,
who cares what our bodies did then?

> We walked hand in hand in small town streets
> and whispered "gay" in those underground days.
> We convinced our families it was just a phase
> and wondered ourselves how much we'd pay
> for Bohemian pranks and dancing and lust.
> We didn't worry overmuch, and what we felt
> was sweet as it passed and profound as it stayed
> through the days and nights of our separate lives.

Only I remember what our bodies did then.
And now I know: bodies go.

At the Supermarket

Still tall though stooped, he moves down
aisles of fruit, tapping melons, weighing apples
selectively. A white-haired man wearing chinos
with one leg rolled as if for a bicycle propped outside
(not likely today), he peers at the produce and
steers the metal cart cautiously, in retirement doing
what his wife did before. He performs tasks
as carefully as he did those his lab demanded,
fixing his scientist's eye on fruit and vegetables
and the sides of cans—giving his all and ignoring as ever
fellow humans, even friends, who smile at the old man.

Alzheimer Moment

"It's under there." "Where?"
"The grass is under the snow."
"Oh. I know grass green and brown.
Green, brown—and white?"
"Yes, the white, that's snow."
"Thank you for saying so. I had
the green, brown, white. I'd lost—
snow."

Another time I may say winter, spring,
summer, fall. For now it's enough we stand,
two women at a window, and croon together
"Snow!"

Old and Admirable

The shirts I wear in summer I've worn
for ten years. Slacks I wear I've had
somewhat longer. Winter things outlast
even these, being loose and being wool.

Once I admired a friend's overcoat
he was hanging where he'd watch it
while we dined out. "I've had it," he said,
"since high school." That day he was forty
or so, a professor like me, and pleased to be
wearing what was old and still admirable.

Police Log

Asked to identify her mugger,
she said, "He was beautiful."
She had watched him run away,
studied his grace from where
she lay not quite out, not quite here.
The loss of her purse seemed, she said,
worth it to see what she saw.

Oh, dear—the police didn't know
how to take an old lady's praise
of one who had shoved her aside
for what little he found she possessed.
They wrote on the blotter the date,
the time, and her state: "confused."

I Stopped Telling Jokes

I stopped telling jokes when Ludmilla died—
couldn't do voices any more, those voices
that brought her to laughs and to tears.
"Oh no—oh yes—I see," she'd say, prompting
the gestures, the pauses for effect.
I'd try telling jokes again, but I fear
they'd lack cadences of pleasure we shared.
What's the point? My friend is gone who
laughed at all my silliness. Of course,
she may be telling my stories now to I. B. Singer,
maybe to Perelman or Oscar Levant. She can have them,
the jokes. I have the memory of her inimitable laugh.

Elegy

Her song gone, the bird lies
on the road like a shuttlecock,
feathers angled stiff and stark,
stuck in tar. Done in by wind
or worse, the bird lies still.

When music's gone, grace goes.
When life leaves, there's love
—still.

Rosa

She turned because I stamped,
    deaf old dog.
She hadn't half a notion why
    anything mattered.
Nor do I.

'Cause She's Old

My neighbor tells me Rosa's respected by other dogs
"'cause she's old." What do they do, I wonder,
to show respect? Give her leftovers? She'd like that
a lot. Sniff her none-too-pleasant breath with pleasure?
That would be a gesture not accorded her at home.

She stumbles abroad, visits pups without invitation,
and she's respected—or so I'm told. Rosa, who sees
less and less and eats more and more, knows she wants
something—and barks to have it. But what? Does she
know? Perhaps she barks for respect from those dogs
and gets it "'cause she's old." Good for you, Rosa.

Tell about the Good Times

Tell about the good times please,
when mewling meant contentment, not pain;
when stumbling meant falling, and falling
wasn't fear. When Rosa was young she rolled
on her mother and sighed, full of milk.
She played in the rough and tumble rapture
of pups in a tangle electric with life.
Tell about her good times please.

In Old Age

Rosa has added to her barking repertoire
a kind of muffled crying, like the sound
of a muted French horn. Clearly in a minor key.
Where her barking—unheard by her, deaf old dear—
seems to shatter windows, this music quietly rises
in uncanny phrases of sadness as she reaches
the end of her song, the end of her long life.

When I weep at her passing, I'll try to recall
the sounds I hear from her now to reproduce them
for the empty air.

Caesar

When my dog Caesar throws a fit,
we comfort him—though he's unaware
of fit or comforter—hold him close
and tell him words he cannot hear.
Or so we guess from his empty stare.
Where does he go then? And how
does he find his way back?

For a Dog Named Amelia

It scares me when I see her eyes, see them
clearly. Bangs should keep them secret,
sweetly recondite. Exposed, they fix me
with a curious stare that startles me.
Her soul's there suddenly, and I'm allowed
to know in passing what animates my dog,
my little friend. All I can do is hold her
close and tell her "There, there."

Fin

Some cat some day
will walk away
in a state of hauteur
when I'm not here.
But now, my Fin,
you walk the new
mown green, stalking
your own intentions.
And I am jealous
of that day
in a way you
cannot be,
jealous of a time
when we have gone,
woman and cat,
leaving the sward—
and so much more—
to others.

Cats: A Love Story

She touched his face. She touched Hugo's
face. With lowered head and curling tongue,
she touched him. Small gesture that, but not
for her. A housebound cat, she worships Hugo
who roams. When he comes home, she runs to show
she's here. *His* move is usually languidly away.
Today he stood imperious while Dolly moved her
pretty tilted head to touch her Hugo's face.

Preacher

for Cynthia Packard

The day Jimmy Baldwin died
the fox got my one black hen,
left the red and black & white
alone.
I hear his cat Preacher,
the only cat he'd ever named,
disappeared that day
not to return.
What does it mean?
Anything? Not much.
I miss my chick,
and Cynthia knows
where her cat's at.

At the Feast of Seeds

A male cardinal, followed by his drabber mate,
ate at our feeder today. They were chased away
by bossy jays, then replaced by busy finches
in search of a turn at the feast of seeds.
Then greedy grosbeaks, then cardinals again.
    The movement seemed choreographed
      in colors designed to delight my eye.
But the birds, alertly unconcerned,
danced for no one. They simply ate.

Deconstructing Ladybird/Ladybug

The Brits say *birds*, and we say *bugs*
(or so I'm told by the *O. E. D.*).
Ladybirds or ladybugs, they're
everywhere this spring. Where flies
have stumbled other years, ladybugs scoot.
Separating shiny backs into wings, they go
in search of—what? Aphids, I'm told.
And maybe the eggs of flies? Very few
flies this spring. "Predatory beetles. . .
the most common being brownish red,
with black spots." It doesn't end there,
for Webster says some call a ladybird
"Our Lady's bird." The Virgin Mary's
own bird? What has she to do with this
pretty little bug of a bird? And why,
I ask you, do the French call it "Bête à
Bon Dieu" and ask it, "Bête à Bon Dieu,
fera-t-il beau Dimanche?" Will it be
fair on Sunday? There's another clue:
Sunday. "Never kill a ladybug. Bad luck."
It may be holy. God's own.

But why as kids did we sing, "Ladybug, ladybug,
fly away home?" Where was home for such as she?
She? Did we care to know if a concept called home
meant a gentleman bug somewhere? Where's a ladybug's
home? And what about lines that come after our urging
the little bug home? "Your house is on fire. Your
children all gone." What did it mean sending her on
to a place in flames? And the children "gone." Gone
in what sense? Escaped? Dead? What did we fear?
Or did we just prate, "Ladybug, ladybug, fly away home.
Your house is on fire. Your children all gone."

One revisionist tale adds words
that save a child named Ann who's
"crept under the warming pan." Another
announces the children aren't gone;
they're asleep, "snug in their nest,"
where their mother joins them at last
and at last finds rest. Not for me
these new endings. I'm not a child of today.
I won't be protected from knowing the house
is in flames and the children all gone.
Oh, I'll wonder about bug or bird
and Mary or God—and I'll ask, "Will it be fair
on Sunday?"